First Science

Watch it Grow!

Editorial planning: Serpentine Editorial
Scientific consultant: Dr. J.J.M. Rowe

Designed by The R & B Partnership
Illustrator: David Anstey
Photographer: Peter Millard

Additional photographs:
ZEFA 6; Julian Rowe 10, 11 (top and bottom),
12, 16, 18 (top and bottom), 19 (top and bottom),
21, 23, 30 (top), 31 (top); Eye Ubiquitous 20, 26;
Bruce Coleman 28; The Hutchison Library 29;
Chris Fairclough Colour Library 30 (bottom).

Library of Congress Cataloging-in-Publication Data

Rowe, Julian.
    Watch it grow! / by Julian Rowe and Molly Perham.
      p.   cm. — (First science)
    Includes index.
    ISBN 0-516-08141-1
    1. Growth (Plants) — Juvenile literature. 2. Plants — Juvenile literature.
3. Growth (Plants) — Experiments — Juvenile literature. 4. Plants —
Experiments — Juvenile literature. [1. Plants. 2. Growth (Plants) — Experiments.
3. Experiments.] I. Perham, Molly. II. Title. III. Series: First science (Chicago, Ill.)
QK731.R64 1994
581.3—dc20   94-12258
                                                  CIP
                                                   AC

Watch it Grow!

Julian Rowe
and Molly Perham

CHILDRENS PRESS®

CHICAGO

Contents

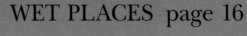

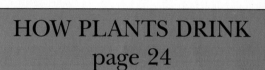

 SAFETY WARNING
Activities marked with this symbol require the presence
and help of an adult. Plastic should always be used
instead of glass. Take special care near water.

Traveling seeds

If you blow dandelion seeds, they float away in the air. New dandelion plants may grow from the seeds where they land on the ground.

The wind can spread seeds far and wide.

Some seeds are spread by birds and other animals. Gardeners and farmers plant seeds where they want the plants to grow.

Sprouting

Seeds need water to sprout. Put some seeds on wet cotton balls and put the jar in a warm place.

Soon the seeds will start to sprout. This is called germination.

Alfalfa or radish seeds sprout in a few days.

Grow some seeds

Materials: A plate, alfalfa or radish seeds, and paper towels.

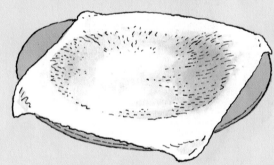

1. Put two paper towels on the plate.

2. Wet the towels and sprinkle on the seeds.

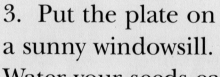

3. Put the plate on a sunny windowsill. Water your seeds each day.

See how the shoots grow toward the light.

Seeds and fruit

These fruits have seeds inside them.
Apple seeds are the seeds of the apple tree.

Many plants produce fruit that is good to eat.

The juicy flesh of these grapes and oranges protects the seeds inside.

Sun power

Plants need water and light to grow.

They use the energy of the sun to change water and air into sugar in their leaves. This provides the plant with food.

These sunflowers face the sun. Their heads turn to follow the sun across the sky.

Grow sunflowers

Materials: Sunflower seeds and a trowel.

1. Dig some holes in a sunny part of the garden. Ask first!

2. Put two or three seeds in each hole.

3. Cover them with soil and water them.

How tall do your sunflowers grow?

Watch them turn to face the sun!

Water and soil

Growing plants take in water from the soil. Their roots help the soil to hold the water so that it doesn't drain away.

In some soils the water drains away easily.

Green plants also take in minerals from the soil. These minerals help the plants to grow.

Plant seeds in soil

Materials: A seed tray, soil or growing compost, and a package of seeds.

1. Fill the tray half-full with soil.

2. Spread the seeds evenly over the soil.

3. Sprinkle more soil on top.

4. Put the seed tray in a warm, sunny place.

5. Water the soil every day.

How long does it take your seedlings to sprout?

Wet places

Some plants like to grow in water.

Water lilies float on top of lakes and ponds. They get the minerals they need from the water.

Air trapped in their underwater stems makes them float.

You can find all kinds of plants in a pond.

Fish and small pond animals eat waterweeds.
Water birds nest among the reeds.

The animals and plants need each other to live.

The seasons

Plants follow a regular pattern through the seasons.

The chestnut tree grows new leaves and flowers in the spring.

In summertime, prickly fruits appear. The burs inside are the seeds of the chestnut tree.

When autumn comes, the leaves of the chestnut tree change color and fall to the ground.

The prickly seed cases split open and burs drop to the ground. From these seeds, new trees may grow.

Food from plants

We need plants to provide us with food.

In Sri Lanka, rice is a main food. The rice plants grow best in fields flooded with water. These fields are called rice paddies.

In many parts of the world, wheat is grown for making flour and bread.

Seeds are sown in the spring, and the wheat is harvested at the end of summer.

Water your plants!

Without water, plants dry up and die. Plants growing indoors must be watered regularly.

Outdoor plants are watered by the rain.

Where there is not enough rain, farmers must provide their crops with water.

How plants drink

Plants take in the water they need through their roots.
The water travels up inside the stem to the leaves.

You can see how this happens by standing some celery in colored water.

After half an hour cut the stalk and see how far the colored water has traveled.

Grow some bean sprouts

Materials: A large plastic jar, a piece of thin cloth, a rubber band, and a cup of mung beans.

1. Put the beans in the jar.

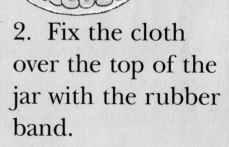

2. Fix the cloth over the top of the jar with the rubber band.

3. Fill the jar with water to soak the beans.

4. Pour the water out and put the jar on a sunny windowsill.

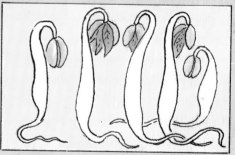

5. Do this each day until the bean sprouts are big enough to eat.

Rain and clouds

A cloud is made up of tiny drops of water. When it rains they fall to Earth.

The rain waters plants and collects in rivers and lakes.

Sometimes you can see water vapor rising from a lake into the air.

You can see a cloud of water vapor rising from the hot water in this bowl. The air above the bowl is cooler than the water.

This glass is cold. You can see how the water vapor has turned into droplets of water.

Clouds form in cold air from water vapor.

Dry places

In deserts, very little rain falls. Sometimes it rains only once in seven years.

An oasis is a place where plants can grow because there is water from an underground river or a spring.

Cacti are well adapted to life in the desert. When rain falls, they store the water in their stems. Some have roots that spread over a wide area to catch as much rain as possible.

Think about... growing

Gardeners use greenhouses to make plants grow faster and bigger. Heat from the sun is trapped under the glass.

The giant sequoia is one of the biggest plants in the world. It can grow as high as a tall building.

Bees and butterflies carry pollen from one flower to another. This pollination helps a flowering plant to produce new seed.

A potted plant uses up all the minerals in the soil. These must be replaced to keep the plant healthy.

INDEX